PHILOSOPHERS OF THE SPIRIT

CHUANG TZU

PHILOSOPHERS OF THE SPIRIT

CHUANG TZU

Edited by

Robert Van de Weyer

Hodder & Stoughton
LONDON   SYDNEY   AUCKLAND

British Library Cataloguing in Publication Data:
A record for this book is available from the British Library.

ISBN 0 340 69466 1

Typeset in Monotype Columbus by
Strathmore Publishing Services, London N7.

Printed and bound in Great Britain by
Mackays of Chatham PLC, Chatham, Kent.

Hodder and Stoughton Ltd,
A division of Hodder Headline PLC,
338 Euston Road, London NW1 3BH

CONTENTS

SERIES INTRODUCTION

The first task of philosophers is to ask questions – the questions which lurk in all our minds, but which, out of fear or confusion, we fail to articulate. Thus philosophers disturb us. The second task of philosophers is to try and answer the questions they have asked. Since their answers are inevitably only partial, philosophers both interest and infuriate us. Their third and most important task is to stimulate and inspire us to ask questions and seek answers for ourselves.

The human psyche or spirit has always been the main – although not the only – focus of philosophy. Inevitably when the psyche is explored, the gap between religion and philosophy rapidly narrows. Indeed for philosophers in the more distant past there was no gap at all, since philosophy was an aspect of theology and even mysticism. Although religious institutions are now quite weak, questions of spiritual philosophy are being asked more keenly and urgently than ever.

This series is an invitation to readers, with no philosophical training whatever, to grapple with the great philosophers of the spirit. Most philosophy nowadays is served in the form of brief summaries, written by commentators. Each of these books contains an introduction to the life and ideas of the philosopher in question. But thereafter the reader encounters the philosopher's original words – translated into modern English. Usually the words are easy to follow; sometimes they are more difficult. They are never dull, always challenging, and frequently entertaining.

INTRODUCTION

The Taoist Genius

By its nature Taoism, one of the great spiritual philosophies of China, is relatively indifferent to the details of history; and it does not recognise a founder, since it regards its principles as eternal. Nonetheless, for the past two thousand years it has acknowledged two books as expressing most fully these principles. The first is the *Tao Te Ching,* which is usually attributed to Lao Tzu, but is probably an anthology of wise sayings. This book, which is quite short, has enjoyed a wide circulation in the West in recent decades. The second, which is much longer, is *The Book of Chuang Tzu.* He almost certainly did not write it himself. But he undoubtedly existed; and the book is a compilation of his wit and wisdom.

There is no adequate English translation for the word 'Tao'. The best equivalent is the Way, implying that Taoism is not a set of doctrines and beliefs, but rather an attitude, and thence a pattern of life. Chuang Tzu never tries to define the Way, nor explain it. But in the course of his book a number of connected themes emerge. The most striking is that those who follow the Way are free. They are not bound by moral rules of right and wrong. They are not attached to power, wealth or status. They are not tied to conventional ideas of joy and sorrow, happiness and sadness. They are even indifferent to life and death. Thus they are not subject to any of the anxieties and aspirations which preoccupy most human beings, constraining their thoughts and actions.

Yet balancing this sense of freedom is acute awareness of the inherent nature of all creatures, and hence their destinies. Those who follow the Way seek to attain inner harmony, by living in total accord with their own natures, and by accepting meekly whatever events destiny brings. Equally they respect the differing natures of other human beings, and of the countless species of animal, plant and bird with whom humans share the earth. No attempt should be made to force creatures to live against their natures; and judgements of right and wrong are entirely contingent on what suits, or does not suit, a creature.

The primary fruit of following the Way is calmness. Followers are no longer anxious to alter their circumstances in order to satisfy transient wants and needs; but they are content with whatever befalls them. A second, and rather surprising, fruit is that they tend to acquire great skill and artistry. According to Chuang Tzu, the enemy of skill is self-consciousness, induced by pride and the desire for success; this inhibits people's inherent abilities. But when people follow the Way, they forget the self, and so their abilities can flourish.

* * *

The only historical details we have of Chuang Tzu are from Chapter 63 of the *Historical Records,* compiled by Ssu Ma Chien in the first century BC. According to this account, Chuang Tzu was born and grew up in a place called Meng, which probably lay south of the Yellow River in present-day Honan. Ssu Ma Chien gives the names of two local kings, during whose reigns Chuang Tzu lived; and by identifying these kings in other historical documents, we can infer that Chuang Tzu died around 310 BC, probably as quite an old man. We are also told that, in addition to writing a large book, he once served as 'an official in the lacquer garden'. This peculiar detail suggests that Chuang Tzu was well-educated, and for a period was employed by the king. But while his title may have implied that he was responsible for one of the royal lacquer groves, he was probably more valued for his philosophical insight. However, we know from his own writings that this phase in his career was brief, and that he soon became a freelance philosopher, moving from place to place. And his writings, though modest in this respect, give the impression that he gradually acquired a large band of disciples, who travelled with him.

In Chuang Tzu's time, China was not yet a single state. On the contrary, it consisted of a number of separate kingdoms which were frequently at war with one another, each trying to seize more territory for itself. This political conflict was mirrored by philosophical conflict, with several philosophical schools vying for royal patronage and popular support. The schools broadly fell into two camps, the Taoist and the Confucian. The Taoist emphasis on freedom enjoyed greater favour with lower social groups, appealing to artisans and peasants. The Confucian schools, all of which claimed Confucius as their founder and guide, stressed the importance of social order and solidarity, to be achieved by strict adherence to moral norms and by deference to those in positions of authority. This naturally had greater appeal to people of higher rank; and most kings, as well as many merchants and landowners, prided themselves on having Confucian philosophers in their households, to act as advisers.

Although the dominant tone of his book is serene and tranquil, Chuang Tzu displays considerable passion in his contempt for Confucianism and for those who promulgate it. His particular hatred is reserved for the junior bureaucrats employed by the king, who, having begun to climb the social ladder, use

Confucian philosophy to justify their petty snobberies and their maltreatment of the poor. One can guess that this hatred prompted him to resign his own position as a bureaucrat. The hatred appears to have been mutual. In various places in his book incidents are recorded where Confucians try to confound Chuang Tzu and make him look foolish. Nonetheless, Chuang Tzu maintained friendly relations with one of the senior ministers at the royal court, called Hui Shih, who was a Confucian scholar. The two men enjoyed many lively debates; and when Hui Shih died, Chuang Tzu confessed to missing such a worthy and intelligent opponent.

During his lifetime and after his death Chuang Tzu's reputation and writings spread rapidly across China. Indeed for several decades his fame seems to have rivalled Confucius himself. But when China became unified about a century after Chuang Tzu's death, the imperial rulers regarded Taoism as dangerously subversive; and those who declared themselves openly as followers of the Way were cut off from any employment or preferment by the State. Thus Taoism went into eclipse, surviving only as a private religion; and the books of Lao Tzu and Chuang Tzu had to be circulated secretly. Since that time the popularity of Taoism has waxed and waned, depending on the political and economic fortunes of China itself. Thus when China broke up again into warring kingdoms in the third century CE. Taoism experienced a revival and Chang Tzu's fame was renewed. But when three hundred years later unity was restored, Taoism was pushed back into the shadows. In times of uncertainty and disorder Taoism's stress on freedom and natural harmony has particular appeal – which explains the growing popularity of Taoism in the West.

* * *

The Book of Chuang Tzu, as it has come down to us, was edited by Kuo Hsiang, early in the fourth century CE. He probably collected all the writings attributed to Chuang Tzu which were then in circulation and divided them into three parts. The first part, consisting of seven chapters, are the records made by his immediate disciples of his teachings – these are usually called the Inner Chapters. The second part, consisting of the next fifteen chapters, are the products of those who continued to adhere to his teaching after his death, and wrote down what they could remember of his ideas; these are called the Outer Chapters. The third part, consisting of eleven chapters, is a miscellany of teachings which seem to be inspired by Chuang Tzu, but whose origins were uncertain. Not surprisingly scholars have continued to this day to debate this classification; and may have pointed out that there is little difference in style and content between the three parts.

Some have compared *The Book of Chuang Tzu* with a travelogue: it moves from place to place, recording encounters and conversations as they occur. Certainly this is the superficial impression. But in fact there is more subtlety to the arrangement of the material than this suggests. Many of the chapters have a dominant theme, which is introduced at the beginning, and then played with several variations later. In addition, each chapter contains a number of sub-themes, which are mostly the dominant themes from other chapters. There is also considerable variation in the forms in which the teachings are presented. Sometimes Chuang Tzu addresses the reader directly; he may speak at length, exploring a particular point in detail, or he may use short aphorisms which lodge in the mind. At other times we witness Chuang Tzu – usually presented in the third person as a 'wise man' – meeting people and responding to their questions. And occasionally we are given little stories, which illustrate Chuang Tzu's teaching.

The historian Ssu Ma Chien estimated that *The Book of Chuang Tzu* contains 100,000 words. An English translation of Kuo Hsiang's edition is about precisely this length. And it has to be admitted that it is very variable in quality. As a result it has not enjoyed the readership in the West that its ideas deserve. The present book contains about one sixth of the original. In those extracts the full range of

Chuang Tzu's thought has been preserved, but at the same time repetition and obscurity have largely been eliminated. Kuo Hsieng's chapter headings have been kept, and extensive extracts from all seven of the Inner Chapters have been included – plus extracts from a number of the later chapters.

To the logical and practical western mind, much of Chuang Tzu's teaching is an affront; and for this reason it is sometimes hard to grasp. He relished contradictions; and he loved to undermine conventional wisdom. Chuang Tzu did not admire scholarly argument, and reviled those who thought wisdom could be acquired through it. At the same time he did not want people to accept his teaching uncritically. In effect his book invites us to be his companions on the Way, sharing his mental, emotional and spiritual experiences. The book thus should be read as an acceptance of this invitation.

ROBERT VAN DE WEYER

I

WANDERING WHERE YOU WILL

from *The Book of Chuang Tzu*, Chapter 1

If water is not deep enough, it does not have the ability to carry a large boat. Pour a cup of water into a small hollow in the floor. A scrap of paper will float on it. But set the cup itself in the water, and it will push through the water and rest on the floor.

* * *

If you go out into the countryside near your home, you may pack only a single meal to take with you, knowing that this will be sufficient to keep your stomach full. If you were to travel a hundred miles, you would need to take enough food for several days. If you were to travel a thousand miles, you would pack enough food for three months, What does this tell us? A little understanding takes us a little way; greater understanding takes us a longer way.

* * *

The morning mushroom knows nothing of the dusk and the dawn. The cicada knows nothing of the spring and autumn. They have short lives. To the south of Chu there is a vast creature which counts five hundred years as one spring, and five hundred years as one autumn. Long ago there was a giant tree called Chun, whose flowers were in bloom for eight thousand years. They are examples of long lives. There is a man called Peng Tsu who is famous for his great age. Many people envy him, and would also like to live to a great age. Isn't that pitiful?

* * *

In the north there is a dark sea called Heaven's Pool. In it there lives a fish which is several thousand miles wide, and longer than anyone can measure. This creature is called Vest. There is also a bird called Roc, whose back is like a mountain, and whose wings are like clouds filling the sky. This bird rises up like a whirlwind, soaring through the clouds until its shoulders touch the sky's blueness; then it travels south into the darkness.

The little quail laughs at this bird, saying: 'Where do you think you are going? I give a great leap and fly upwards, but I never rise higher than a few feet, before I come fluttering down amidst the weeds and thorns. And that's the best kind of flying anyway! So where does that creature think he is going?'

This is what distinguishes the small from the great.

* * *

A man who is intelligent enough to fulfil the duties of one office, whose conduct is good enough to impress one community, who possesses enough virtue to please one ruler – who, in short, is moderately gifted – is likely to be very proud of himself. But those who are wise would burst out laughing at such a man. The whole world can praise someone who is wise, and that person will not be goaded into greater activity. The whole world can condemn someone who is wise, and that person will not mope. He draws a clear distinction between the inner and outer realms, and he can therefore distinguish true glory and disgrace from their illusory forms. He thus does not care about the world's opinion.

* * *

The perfect person has no self. The holy person has no merit. The wise person has no fame.

* * *

An emperor wished to hand his empire over to a hermit. 'When the sun and the moon have already come out,' the emperor said, 'is it not a waste of fuel to go on burning torches? When the rains have started to fall, is it not a waste of water to continue irrigating the fields? Now that you are present, it is foolish for such an imperfect person as me to remain emperor. If you took the throne, then all would be well.'

The hermit replied: 'You govern the world well. What motive could I have in taking your place? Acquiring fame for myself? But fame is nothing compared with reality; it is the guest of reality – and I have no desire to be a guest. A bird uses only one branch in the entire forest to make her nest. A mole drinks only one bellyful from the entire river. Go home, my lord, and forget about this matter. I have no interest in ruling the empire. Even if the cook does not run the kitchen perfectly, the priest does not jump up and take over.'

* * *

There is a wise and holy man who lives far away on a mountain. His skin is as white as snow. He eats nothing, but lives off the wind and dew. He climbs the clouds and rides on lightning. He travels beyond the boundaries of the world. His spirit is so pure that he can heal all diseases and make every harvest abundant.

You may refuse to believe that such a person exists, and dismiss all talk of him as nonsense. But we cannot expect a blind man to appreciate beautiful patterns, or a deaf man to enjoy bells and drums. And blindness and deafness are not confined to the body; they affect the soul as well.

* * *

The man of virtue can hold all existence in his hand, and roll it into one.

* * *

A man invented a recipe for making a salve, which could prevent hands from becoming chapped in cold weather. He and his family just used it for themselves. One day a traveller called at the man's house and observed him using the salves. He purchased the recipe for five gold coins. The traveller took it to the King of Wu, whose troops were losing many battles in winter, because their hands were too chapped to hold their swords. At the king's instructions the traveller gave the salve to all the troops; and instead of losing battles, they won them. As a reward the king gave the traveller a large area of his kingdom – while the man who invented the salve only had five gold coins, which were soon spent.

Value your own ideas highly, and put them to the best use.

* * *

Look at the weasel. It is small, but it is so agile it can catch as many rats as it can eat. Look at the yak. The only thing it can do is be big, Yet the weasel ends up being caught in a trap or a net; while the yak lives in peace, and dies of old age.

If you are useless, at least you won't suffer grief or pain.

2
MAKING ALL THINGS EVEN

from *The Book of Chuang Tzu*, Chapter 2

A wise man sat upright in his chair. He was staring into the distance and breathing very slowly; his body was absolutely still. A disciple who was standing nearby exclaimed: 'The man who sat down on the chair is no longer present. His body has become like a withered tree and his mind like dead ashes. He has lost himself. How can this happen?'

The wise man turned to the young disciple, and said: 'Your question is apt. I have indeed lost myself. Do you truly understand that? You hear the pipes of the people, but not the pipes of the earth. And even if you hear the pipes of the earth, you do not hear the pipes of heaven.'

* * *

True understanding is wide and serene; superficial understanding is cramped and busy. Words of wisdom are concise and dear; foolish words are petty and mean.

When we sleep, our spirits roam the earth; when we are awake, our bodies are busy. We become entangled in everything we encounter. Day by day we are caught up in conflicts, some great, some devious, some trivial.

Small troubles unsettle our minds, making us anxious. Large troubles stun and overwhelm us.

We rush into action, convinced we know right from wrong. We cling to our convictions, as if they were sacred promises, certain that they will lead us to victory. But our convictions wither and fall, like leaves in autumn.

Assumption = conviction

* * *

We identify ourselves with our bodies. From birth until death we cling on to our bodies. Sometimes our bodies are in conflict with others, sometimes in harmony. We go through life like galloping horses, unable to stop. Is not this pathetic?

We work hard until the end of our days. And what do we accomplish? We exhaust ourselves, and yet we are incapable of resting. And do we ever appreciate what we have done? We are pitiful creatures.

'I'm not dead yet,' we cry. But what good is that? The body gradually decays, followed by the mind – is not this tragic?

Human life has always been ridiculous. Or is it just me who is ridiculous – and everyone else sane?

* * *

If you allow your mind to guide you, then you are never without a teacher. Why do people think that only those who understand the process of change within the mind can be teachers? Even an idiot has the knowledge to be his own teacher. But if you do not listen to your mind, and instead follow arbitrary rules of right and wrong, then you are like someone who says: 'I set off for a certain town today, and arrived there yesterday.' You are claiming these moral rules have objective existence; yet they are illusions.

* * *

Words are not just like wind. Words work because they say something. Yet if we cannot define a word's meaning, we cannot be sure what it is saying; and the only method of definition is to use other words. People presume that words are different from the cheeps of baby birds. But is there really a difference?

How is it that the Way is so obscured, that we must have definitions of truth and falseness? What has clouded our words, so that we are so confused?

* * *

Every object is simultaneously 'this' and 'that'. I can only look at objects through my own eyes; I cannot look through other people's eyes. So through my eyes I may regard an object as 'this'; but another person may regard the same object as 'that'. Thus we can say that 'this' and 'that' are born out of one another.

But where there is birth, there is also death; and where there is death, there is birth. Similarly where there is possibility, there is impossibility; and where there is impossibility, there is possibility. In the same way, where people recognise right, they also recognise wrong – and vice versa.

The wise person cannot proceed by opposite, but by the Way. On the Way this and that contain one another; so do right and wrong. Does that mean that these categories disappear? A state in which there are no opposites is called the pivot of the Way. This pivot is at the centre of the circle of the Way, which has no beginning and no end.

* * *

What exists, exists; what does not exist, does not exist. The Way is made because we walk on it; and because we walk on it, we call it the Way. Why is this so? Because it is so. How could it not be so? If it *were* not so. Everything has what is both innate and necessary; nothing exists which does not have innate and necessary qualities.

Take a stalk of wheat, and a pillar. Take a leper and a beautiful maiden. Take something great, and something trivial. Take something humorous, and something dull. Take something strange, and something normal. The Way makes them all alike. In their difference is their completeness; in their completeness is their difference.

Through the Way all things are seen as one, regardless of their completeness or their difference. Those who follow the Way are able to see the unity of all things.

* * *

Do not wear out your brain trying to work out the unity of all things. This is called 'three in the morning'. What do I mean by 'three in the morning'? A monkey trainer, handing out acorns to his monkeys, said: 'You get three in the morning and four at night.' This made all the monkeys furious. 'Very well,' he replied, 'you get four in the morning and three at night.' The monkeys were delighted. There was no change in the reality behind the words; yet the attitude of the monkeys changed from anger to joy. Let attitudes change as they will. The wise person takes no particular attitude, but harmonises all attitudes.

* * *

There is order in chaos, and certainty in doubt. The wise are guided by this order and certainty.

* * *

There is what is, and there is what is not. It is not easy to confirm that what is not, is not. This is a statement.

Yet I do not know whether my statements affirm what is, or affirm what is not.

* * *

There is nothing greater than the tip of a hair; the greatest mountain is no greater. No one lives longer than a dead child, even the oldest man that ever lived. Heaven and earth were created at the same time that I was. All life and I are one.

* * *

The Way has no boundaries; words do not have constant meanings. But because people want to say, 'this is …', boundaries were created. Let me tell you about these boundaries. There is left and right; there are theories and debates; there are divisions and disagreements; there are victories and defeats. The wise person does not deny these boundaries, but pays no attention to them.

THE SWORD OF CONCEPTUALISATION

* * *

Those who are perfect are pure spirit. They do not feel the heat of burning deserts, nor the cold of mountain streams. They are not frightened by lightning which can split open mountains, nor by storms which shake the oceans. They ride the clouds, using the sun and the moon as their steeds, and they wander freely across the world. Neither death nor life concern them; nor are they interested in right and wrong, profit and loss.

* * *

Do not strive for wisdom. Striving for wisdom is like counting your chickens before the eggs are hatched, or looking at a plate and imagining a roasted fowl. I am going to speak randomly, and I want you to listen randomly. How can people become wise enough to sit beside the sun and moon, and embrace the universe? Wise people harmonise themselves with all things; they do not try to resolve confusion and muddle; they ignore status and power. Ordinary people try to be intelligent, and struggle to impose order; wise people are happy to be stupid and ineffectual.

* * *

Those who dream of a drunken feast may weep when morning comes; while those who dream of weeping may go hunting when morning comes. When we dream, we do not know we are dreaming. Indeed while we are dreaming, we may even try to interpret the dream. Only after we awake do we know it was a dream. Some day there will be a great awakening when we realise that everything is a dream. Yet those who lack wisdom are convinced they are truly awake; they think they understand what is happening; they think the king is really the king, and the servants are really servants.

* * *

Suppose that you and I had an argument. If you won the argument, would it mean that you were right and I wrong? If you lost, would I be right and you wrong? Does one of us have to be right, and one wrong? Or is it possible for both of us to be right, and both of us wrong? Perhaps we could acknowledge that neither of us knows the answer; nor does anyone else.

* * *

Where there is a dispute, it is foolish to hope that one voice will resolve it. Instead allow differing views to co-exist, recognising that they have equal value. Then allow the process of constant change to continue unimpeded. Let the months and the years pass. Gradually the differing views will harmonise. This is because right is not right, wrong is not wrong. If right were really right, it would differ so clearly from what is wrong, that there would be no dispute.

* * *

I once dreamt I was a butterfly. I fluttered around, enjoying myself and going where I pleased. I didn't know I was me. Then suddenly I awoke, and there I was, solid and unmistakable. But as I reflected I could not tell whether I was a butterfly who was dreaming it was me, or me who had dreamt I was a butterfly.

3
LIVING IN THE WORLD

from *The Book of Chuang Tzu*, Chapter 4

Do you know what destroys wisdom, and what is the source of knowledge? Virtue is destroyed by fame; and knowledge comes from argument. In their struggle for fame people beat one another down; and argument is a device they use for this purpose. Thus both fame and knowledge are evil, and you should avoid them.

You may have great virtue and unquestionable sincerity. You may be kind-hearted and indifferent to fame. But if you do not understand how people feel and think, you will do harm, not good. You will try to compel people to be benevolent, by requiring them to listen to sermons on benevolence, and by imposing rules and laws. As a result, despite your good intentions, people will come to hate you. You may want them to be good and happy, but you will make them miserable; and they in turn will make you miserable.

* * *

Certain creatures fly by means of wings; but no

creature flies without wings. People come to know certain things by means of knowledge; but no one comes to know anything without knowledge. Look into the room which is closed, the empty chamber where true light is born. In that room there is serenity and contentment. But if you are not able to relax, and must constantly rush hither and thither, you will not be able to enter. The answer is to live both outside and inside the room. Outside the room, acquire knowledge; inside the room acquire wisdom.

* * *

In all we set out to do, whether great or small, we shall only reach a happy conclusion by following the Way. If you fail, you will suffer the adverse judgement of others. If you succeed, you will disturb your own inner balance. To have no distress whether you fail or succeed – that is the mark of someone truly virtuous.

* * *

There are two great principles in the world; one is destiny, and the other is duty. The love of a child for its parents is destiny; that love is in the child's heart. The service of a subject to his ruler is duty; that service is required by the way the world is ordered. To obey your parents in whatever they ask you to do, is true filial piety. To obey your ruler in whatever he asks you to do, is true loyalty. To nurture your own spirit so that sadness or joy do not move it, and to accept your destiny with contentment and tranquillity – this is true virtue. As the offspring of parents, and as the subject of a ruler, you will at times be compelled to do things which you find unpleasant. But if you forget yourself, and do those things with a willing heart, then you will neither love life nor hate death. Act in that way, and all shall be well.

★ ★ ★

If two people are living close together, they can express their mutual care through their actions. But if they are living far apart, they have to rely on words, carried by messengers, to express their love. To convey the joys and sorrows of life through words alone, is the most difficult task on earth. The good aspects of the joys, and the bad aspects of the sorrows, are easily exaggerated. Thus falsehood, and thence distrust, enters the relationship; and the relationship itself is imperilled. Therefore if you find yourself in this position, only transmit the bald facts; in that way you will probably preserve the relationship.

★ ★ ★

When men get together to pit their strength and compete against one another in sport, they usually begin in a friendly mood, but end in a dark and angry one. And if they continue too long, they resort to all sorts of underhand tricks. Similarly when men get together to drink, they begin in an orderly and restrained manner, but degenerate into rowdiness. And if they continue too long, they start indulging in all sorts of improper amusements.

The same applies to all things. What starts with sincerity, ends with deceit. What starts in simplicity, ends with complexity and confusion.

* * *

Accept whatever happens, and let your spirit move freely. Resign yourself to what cannot be avoided, and nurture your own spirit. Obey your own destiny; it is often very difficult, but it is the only means of attaining serenity.

* * *

Do you know how a tiger trainer can avoid being attacked? He doesn't give the tiger any living thing to eat, for fear that the tiger will learn to enjoy killing. He doesn't give the tiger anything whole to eat, for fear that the tiger will learn to enjoy tearing flesh apart. He gauges the tiger's appetite to ensure that he gives the tiger enough food; and he fully understands its disposition. In short, he teaches the tiger to be gentle by respecting the tiger's nature.

Those trainers who get killed are the ones who defy the nature of their tigers.

* * *

A wise man arrived at a town, accompanied by a young disciple. In the middle of the town stood a huge tree; under its vast shady branches people and animals alike were sheltering from the hot sun. The wise man stared at the tree, lost in admiration.

The young disciple asked the wise man: 'Are you thinking of how many boats could be made from this tree, if it were cut down; how many houses could be built; and how many coffins could be made?'

The wise man replied: 'Boats made from the wood of this tree would sink; houses made from this tree would attract wood beetle; coffins would rot even before they were put in the ground. The tree is useless. That is why it has been allowed to live so long and grow so vast – and provide such shelter. If you can become useless, you will live long, your spirit will expand, and you will give great solace to many people.

* * *

In a certain city a crippled man dwells. His back is bent so his chin rests on his chest; and his legs are bent so he cannot walk straight. He earns enough to fill his belly by sewing and washing clothes. And he earns even more by winnowing and sifting grain, so he can offer food to the poor and to strangers. When the king goes to war, he recruits the able-bodied men as labourers; and the cripple wishes them well. In fact the cripple is the most privileged and secure person in the entire city.

* * *

The future can never arrive; the past can never be reclaimed. When the world follows the Way, wise teachers will have succeeded. When the world has lost the Way, wise teachers can only survive, striving to avoid persecution.

Happiness is as light as a feather, but few people know how to catch it. Unhappiness is as heavy as the earth, and most people are weighed down with it.

* * *

All people understand the use of the useful. But few people understand the use of the useless.

4
SHOWING TRUE VIRTUE

———◆———

from *The Book of Chuang Tzu*, Chapter 5

Birth and death are events of great moment. Yet they
have no effect on those who are wise. The sky may
collapse and the earth may crumble. Yet those who
are wise would not be disturbed. Wise people truly
understand the eternal elements of life, and are not
moved by temporal matters. Wise people know that
some events are destined to occur, and so are part of
the eternal order. ★ ★ ★

If you look at things in terms of their differences, you
see only division. But if you look at things in terms
of their similarities, then you see unity. Wise people
do the latter. Thus they perceive things not only
through their eyes and ears, but also with their spirit.
In this way they can see virtue in all things; and
virtue is always in harmony. In perceiving things as
unified, they regard nothing as success or failure, gain
or loss. Even if they were to lose a foot as they walked
along, they would regard it as no different from a
lump of clay that had fallen off a shoe.

★ ★ ★

When people wish to see their reflections, they do not look into running water; they look into still water. Only that which is still can hold other things still.

* * *

If a mirror is bright, no dust or dirt will settle on it. And if dust or dirt does settle, the mirror is no longer bright. If you live long in the company of virtuous people, you will become free of all faults.

* * *

There are many people who try to excuse their misdemeanours, claiming that they do not deserve to be punished. There are very few people who do not excuse their misdemeanours, and who admit that they deserve punishment. To recognise what is beyond your ability to change, and to be content with this as your destiny – that is truly a sign of virtue.

* * *

I once saw some piglets trying to suckle from their dead mother. After a while the piglets looked up, and then ran away; they had realised that their mother was no longer aware of them, so they did not feel any affinity with her. In loving their mother, they had not loved her body, but the spirit which gave life to the body.

* * *

A certain man says nothing, and he is trusted. He does nothing, and is loved. In fact he is so trusted and loved that people want to hand over their property to him, and their only fear is that he will not accept. They recognise that he is a man of perfect character, even though his virtue has no outward form.

* * *

Death and birth, preservation and loss, failure and success, wealth and poverty, value and lack of value, glory and blame, hunger and thirst, cold and heat – all these are part of the pattern of the world, and are determined by destiny. Day and night follow one another, but wisdom cannot discern their source. Do not allow these variations to disturb your inner harmony; do not let them enter your spirit. If you can balance and enjoy them, have mastery over them and revel in them, sustain your balance day after day, and see the unity of all things – then you possess a perfect character. * * *

Water, when it is still, is perfect. Still water should be the example which we strive to imitate. The fish and plants beneath its surface are safe; and its surface shows no sign of movement. It is an image of virtue. Virtue has no outward signs, yet it protects all that is good.

* * *

Those who are wise regard knowledge as a cure, convention as a glue, virtue as only a means, and skill as the path to profit. They do not hatch great plans, so they have no use for knowledge. They do not make divisions, so they have no use for glue. They have no problems, so they do not need virtue. They have no ambition, so they do not acquire skills.

* * *

Those who are wise may look like other people, but they do not have normal emotions. Since they look like other people, they can mingle with them. But since they do not have normal emotions, they do not worry about right and wrong.

* * *

When I say that wise people do not have normal emotions, I mean that they do not allow their likes and dislikes to have any effect on them. They are content with things as they are, and do not try to change things.

5
LEARNING TRUE WISDOM

from *The Book of Chuang Tzu*, Chapter 6

Wise people understand what they understand, and understand what they do not understand. They use what they understand to increase their understanding of what they do not understand.

* * *

Understanding can only be certain when it has been applied. And it can never predict when an opportunity for application will occur.

* * *

Wise people do not strive to avoid poverty, nor do they strive to attain riches. They do not make grand plans. When they make mistakes, they do not feel regret. When they have success, they do not feel elated. They can scale great heights without becoming frightened. They can become soaked in a storm, and not be anxious about falling ill. They can be burnt by a fire, and not be disturbed by the pain. In short they understand how to walk in the Way.

* * *

LEARNING TRUE WISDOM

Wise people sleep without dreaming, and awake without anxiety. They eat without relishing the food, and they breathe very deeply. Wise people breathe from deep within them, whereas most people breathe with their throats.

* * *

Wise people do not cling on to life, nor do they fear death. When they arrive somewhere, they do not demand attention; and they leave without a fuss. Wherever they go, and whatever befalls them, they remain calm. They do not forget their origins; yet they have no ambitions for the future. When they are given something, they receive it with pleasure; when they hand something on to another person, they do so with equal pleasure.

* * *

Wise people have serene hearts, and tranquil faces. They are as chilly as autumn and as warm as spring. They can display joy or anger as need arises. They act appropriately in all circumstances. They are not curious to know the future.

* * *

Those who take delight in success are not wise. Those who show affection to some, and contempt towards others, are not benevolent. Those who are constantly anxious about the future are not serene. Those who strive to profit from every situation, and to avoid loss, are not gentle. Those who seek the praise of others and conduct themselves in order to win it, are not honourable. Those who do not understand their true selves are not fit to guide others.

* * *

Wise people may appear to be hungry and in want but they demand nothing. Their own conduct is dignified, but they do not pass judgement on those who lack their dignity. They are simple and courteous in their speech and demeanour. They are never ostentatious. They appear content, and smile cheerfully. They willingly do whatever their destiny requires. If they become angry, they may show it on their facial expression, but not in any other way. Usually they are calm, and are at one with their surroundings. They are tolerant of the follies and foibles of others. Nothing inhibits or impedes them from doing what they feel impelled to do. Thus they are content to do nothing, wherever their destiny commends this.

* * *

Wise people accept that life and death are determined by destiny. They are as constant as the succession of night and day. Wise people accept that there are many things which human beings cannot alter, since they are inherent in Nature itself. They regard Nature as their father, and so in love and joy they obey Nature's commands.

* * *

Those who are wise are happy to die young, and equally happy to grow old. They enjoy their youth, and they enjoy their later years. They are models which others can imitate.

* * *

The Way has both reality and expression, but it has no action or form. It can be passed on, but not received. You can obtain it, but not see it. It is rooted in its own self, and has existed for all eternity. It gives life to the human spirit; it gives birth to the universe. It is loftier than the highest mountain, yet it cannot be called high. It is deeper than the deepest ocean, yet it cannot be called deep. It is more ancient than the earth, yet it cannot be called old.

* * *

A certain person has the talent to be wise, yet is not wise; whereas I have little talent, yet have become wise. So I decided to try and teach this person wisdom – after all, I surmised, it should be easy teaching wisdom to someone with talent for it. For three days

I taught him to ignore worldly matters. For nine days I taught him to ignore bodily sensations. For seven days I taught him to regard his own self as unimportant. Then he could see with great clarity. He was able to perceive the unity of past and future, and of life and death. He realised that the end of life is not death, and that coming to birth is not life. He could now understand anything and accept everything. To him all was being destroyed, and all was being created. He was tranquil amidst the struggle.

* * *

I was born when the time was right; and I shall die when the time is right. I am content with whatever occurs between birth and death; neither sorrow nor joy can touch me. I am free from all bonds.

* * *

You dream you're a bird, soaring up into the sky. You dream you're a fish, diving deep into the lake. But do you know for certain when you are dreaming, and when you are awake?

* * *

Contentment produces a genuine smile; and a genuine smile cannot be forced. Do not struggle. Go with the flow of things, and you will find yourself at one with the mysterious unity of the universe.

* * *

I shall summarise my teachings. Wise people perceive the reality of all things, but never pass judgement. Wise people bless all things, but do not regard themselves as benevolent. Wise people possess the ancient teaching, but live in the present. Wise people may be adept at all manner of activities, but take no pride in their skills. So attach yourself to wise people.

6

ENLIGHTENING THE KING

from *The Book of Chuang Tzu*, Chapter 7

The enlightened king looks first at himself and his motives before he enacts a decision. He wants to be certain that his only purpose is to enable things to be as they are supposed to be. A bird is supposed to fly high in the sky when it wants tranquillity. It is in the nature of a mouse to make its home deep in the earth. The enlightened king respects the natures of even the smallest creatures.

* * *

A wise man said to a king: 'Let your heart be simple. Be at one with that which is beyond definition. Let things be as they are. Have no personal views. Then you will govern well.'

* * *

Let me tell about the rule of an enlightened king. His works affect everyone under his rule, yet he seems to do nothing. His authority touches everybody, but he makes no one dependent on him. He shuns fame and glory; he only wants his subjects to fulfil themselves.

He acknowledges that there are many things he cannot understand, and so is cautious in making changes.

* * *

A wise man said to a king: 'Do not hanker after fame. Do not make grand plans. Do not undertake great projects. Do not imagine yourself to be wise. Cherish the talents of your people, but do not try to direct how they are used. Be like a mirror. A mirror does not search for or create things, but welcomes and responds to all that come before it. The king who is like a mirror can win over his people, and will never be harmed.

7
WEBBED TOES

from *The Book of Chuang Tzu*, Chapter 8

Certain people have a piece of skin which webs their toes. This may be quite natural to them. But it does not indicate particular virtue or wisdom. Other people have an additional finger. This too is natural for them, but insignificant. People often associate these physical peculiarities with spiritual qualities. But in truth webbing between the toes, or an additional finger, do not engender any extra love, kindness, justice or harmony. Those who regard these things as important are placing too much emphasis on what the five senses perceive. This only leads to confusion, because the senses receive an unending flow of new perceptions.

* * *

Those who are skilled in debate construct their arguments as a builder constructs a wall, brick by brick. They weave their arguments as a netmaker weaves a net with string.

They love to make their arguments circular. They take delight in observing differences in opinions, and hence causing divisions where none existed. These people walk a hard road, which has many twists and bends, and is constantly uphill. This road is not the Way.

* * *

Those on the Way do not lose their inherent nature. Unity delights them, but division does not disturb them. Shortness pleases them, but length does not tire them.

* * *

The legs of a duck are short; and to lengthen them would cause great pain. The legs of a crane are long; and trying to shorten them would cause much grief. We should not cut what nature makes long; we should not stretch what nature makes short.

* * *

Are benevolence and righteousness inherent qualities in human nature? Look how much anxiety is suffered by those who wish to be kind.

* * *

If one toe is attached to another toe by an extra piece of skin, then trying to separate the two toes will cause tears. If a person has an extra finger, then trying to bite it off will provoke screams. Interfering with what is natural always leads to pain. Those who are bene-volent look at the evils of society, and feel very distressed. Those who are not benevolent add to those evils by pursuing wealth and fame. Thus both benevolence and lack of benevolence cause people to interfere with what is natural.

* * *

That which is naturally curved does not require a template to make it curved. That which is naturally straight does not require a plumb-line to make it straight. A round object does not require a compass. A square object does not require a set-square. Objects which are naturally attached do not require glue. Nature makes everything as it should be; and nothing needs to understand why it is as it is. Everything achieves what is intended, without understanding how it does so. This has always been the case, from the beginning of time until now. Even if you are motivated by benevolence, do not use templates and plumb-lines, compasses and set-squares, or any kind of glue, to change the ways of nature.

* * *

Wisdom has nothing to do with benevolence and righteousness. Wisdom consists in knowing how to live according to one's own nature. Wisdom means being led by the natural forces and energies within the spirit. When I speak about having sharp ears, I do not mean being able to hear external sounds; I mean being able to listen to yourself. When I speak about having sharp eyes, I do not refer to looking at external sights; I refer to looking at yourself. Those who listen to and look at others, but do not listen to and look at themselves, may learn to possess and control others, but will not possess and control themselves. They will be attracted to what others enjoy, but will find no enjoyment in themselves. Such people deceive themselves, and do harm to others.

* * *

The only success that matters is finding and following the Way. The only failure that matters is not finding the Way. Do not try to elevate yourself by practising benevolence and righteousness. Following the Way will teach you sufficient virtue.

8
HORSES' HOOVES

—◆—

from *The Book of Chuang Tzu*, Chapter 9

Horses have hooves so that their feet can grip on frost and snow. They have shaggy hair so they can withstand the cold winds. They eat grass and water, and they like to leap and gallop, because this is their nature. They have no desire to live in grand palaces or magnificent halls.

One day a man said: 'I am going to train horses.' He branded them; he cut their hair; he put shoes on their feet and halters on their heads; and he made them live in stables. Out of ten horses, two quickly died. Then he made them hungry and thirsty, in order that they would gallop faster. He raced them and paraded them in front of large crowds; and he put riders on their backs to whip them. Now more than half the horses are dead.

* * *

The potter moulds clay to make plates, cups and vases. The carpenter cuts wood in order to make furniture. It is the nature of clay to be moulded; it is the nature of wood to be cut. Those who train horses claim that it is the nature of horses to be trained. They are talking nonsense.

* * *

Many who are in positions of authority, treat those under their authority as a horse trainer treats his horses. But those who truly know how to wield authority are not like this.

* * *

If people followed the Way, they would live in harmony with each other and with all animals and birds. They would regard the world and all its bounty as belonging to all, to be enjoyed by all. They would have no distinctions of rank and status. They would be honest in their dealings, and never devious. Individuals would each live according to their own natures, and respect the nature of others.

* * *

Do not listen to those people who claim to be religious. They preach about benevolence; they urge people to strive after righteousness; they fuss over the music to be played at religious rituals; and they constantly want to alter the rituals themselves. They upset people, and make people doubt themselves.

* * *

Horses in the wild are content. They show affection for each other by rubbing necks; they show anger by turning their backs and kicking. This is how horses naturally behave. But when they are harnessed together in order to pull a carriage, they arch their necks, they turn their heads this way and that, they try to spit out the bit and to rid themselves of the reins. They know that they are being compelled to behave unnaturally.

* * *

The people of a certain place were content. They were happy with their homes and fields, and with the food they ate. They did not try to ask why they were content. Then along came a religious teacher. He demanded that they treat him with great reverence. He told them that their behaviour was wrong, and that they should strive for righteousness. And he ordered them to perform many complex rituals. Now the people are discontent, always wanting to make themselves and their situation better.

9
STOLEN BOXES

from *The Book of Chuang Tzu*, Chapter 10

To protect our property from thieves, we are told that we should lock our cases and boxes, and tie straps round our bags. All the world agrees that this is wise. But the clever thief simply picks up our cases, boxes and bags when we are asleep or when we momentarily leave them unattended, and piles them on to his cart. He actually wants the locks and straps to hold, so nothing falls out until he has got his booty back to his house. So what seems wise turns out to be folly.

What am I saying? Actions which the world regard as wise often have the effect of encouraging evil. Worldly wisdom is frequently the partner of selfishness and crime.

* * *

Long ago all the towns and villages in a certain kingdom were in harmony with one another; and even the dogs and cockerels would call greetings from one village to the next. The land was perfectly ploughed each year. Beautiful temples were built to give thanks for the rich harvest. There was no crime in the entire kingdom; and the ancestral wisdom was respected by all.

Then one day a fierce leader from another country arrived with his army, and took over this peaceable nation, killing the old king. But did it really become his kingdom? He retained the old laws, and they continued to be obeyed. And so, although the people regarded him as a thief and a murderer, he lived out his days in peace and safety. The neighbouring kingdoms did not dare criticise or attack him. So for twelve generations his family remained rulers. Is not this an example of people benefitting from wisdom which they themselves despise?

I shall try to explain this. Those who are called wise are in fact storing up spiritual wealth for others who do not deserve it.

* * *

A notorious thief once asked a wise man: 'Can a thief follow the Way?' The wise man replied: 'Every profession has its Way. The thief works out what is worth stealing; this demonstrates his intelligence. He demonstrates his courage by leading his gang when they break into someone's house. And he demonstrates his virtue by being the last to leave. He shows his discernment in deciding which places to raid. And he shows his benevolence when he distributes the spoils equally. These five attributes make a person a great thief.'

* * *

The more that wise rulers and their advisers impose order, the more opportunities they create for thieves. The rulers determine the weights and measures by which foods are to be sold; so thieves learn how to make fake weights and measures. The rulers decree that contracts should be drawn up when two people make agreements; so thieves learn how to make contracts where meaning can be disputed. The rulers urge people to act benevolently towards one another; so thieves learn to use benevolence as a mask for their dishonest schemes.

* * *

One person steals a buckle, and he is executed. Another person steals a country, and he becomes its king.

* * *

Those at the top of the social order are apt to preach benevolence and righteousness to those at the bottom. Yet those at the top have typically stolen their position from others. They are the greatest thieves, because they have stolen the greatest amount of land

and other property. So words about benevolence and righteousness are usually the fruit of robbery.

* * *

If wisdom were abandoned, robbery would cease. If all jade and every pearl were shattered, thieves would have nothing to steal. If sets of accounts and legal contracts were burnt, people would be compelled to be honest and trusting. If weights and measures were all broken, people would have nothing to argue about. If all the laws which rulers have passed were obliterated, the people would once again depend on common sense.

* * *

When people have clear vision, they cannot be duped. When people have alert hearing, they cannot be deceived. When people possess true wisdom, they cannot be fooled. When people possess virtue, they cannot be corrupted.

* * *

Long ago people were content with their lives. They were happy in their work, they enjoyed their food, they took delight in their clothes, and they were at ease in their homes. People had no desire for more territory and did not travel beyond their own borders, so there was peace.

But now people are agitated. They are no longer content with their lot. As a result they are constantly pursuing wisdom. One person exclaims: 'In such and such a place a wise man lives!' So they pack their bags and rush off, neglecting their duties at home. You can see their footprints making tracks from one country to another; and the grooves of the carriages go more than a thousand miles.

* * *

If people search for wisdom, but do not know the Way, then there is confusion. It takes a great deal of practical wisdom to make bows and arrows, nets and hooks. But the result is that the birds fly higher to avoid being shot, and the fish swim deeper to avoid being caught. It takes a great deal of scholarly wisdom to construct an argument; it takes verbal wisdom to speak well; it takes political wisdom to bring enemies to ruin. The world is full of all these kinds of wisdom; and as a result the world is confused.

* * *

People know how to condemn what they dislike. But they do not know how to condemn what is wrong within themselves.

IO

YIN AND YANG

———◆———

from *The Book of Chuang Tzu*, Chapter II

Many have been happy to let nature go its own way.
Some have tried to control nature; and they have
never succeeded.

★ ★ ★

We should not try to interfere with the ways of nature
for fear of spoiling it. We should leave nature alone,
knowing that our attempts to manipulate it would
spoil its innate virtue. If we recognise this virtue, then
we will have no desire to control nature.

★ ★ ★

There was once a time when no one tried to manipulate nature; all animals and birds, and all human
beings, were allowed to live according to their own
natures. The whole world was joyful and filled with
energy. Then a ruler took power who wanted to control people and control all creatures. Soon illness and
disease spread everywhere, and people were miserable. There was neither peace nor happiness. People
were fighting against themselves, so they started
fighting against each other.

★ ★ ★

Are people unduly joyful? They will damage the yin. Are people too angry? They will damage the yang. If the yin and the yang are corrupted – if people do not have the right balance between joy and anger – they become unhappy and restless. They move from one place to another searching for contentment, but do not find it. They make plans to improve their circumstances, but these plans, even if they are fulfilled, do not bring satisfaction. When yin and yang are seriously unbalanced, the climate itself is affected: the seasons do not follow one another in proper order. And justice is turned on its head: the wicked are rewarded by having the highest places in society; while the virtuous are punished by having the lowest places.

* * *

When yin and yang are out of balance, people find happiness in nothing. Do people enjoy what they see? No, because colour disturbs them. Do they enjoy what they hear? No, because sound upsets them. Do people take pleasure in being kind to each other? No, because benevolence revolts them. Do they take pride in behaving correctly? No, because they reject good manners. Do they find peace in religious ritual? No, because they are cynical, regarding rituals as pretence. Do they find tranquillity in music? No, because music remains them of their spiritual malaise. Do they appreciate wisdom? No, because they respect only cleverness.

* * *

So how should a king set about his task of governing his kingdom? He should realise that actionless action is the best course. By this I mean that his action should be in accordance with nature and destiny, not against them. He should thus begin by understanding his own nature and destiny; and then he will be ready to understand the nature and destiny of his kingdom. Those who trust their own natures, can be trusted with the world; those who want to fulfil their own destinies, will want the world to fulfil its destiny.

* * *

Take care with people's hearts. People's hearts should not be pushed down or pulled up. To push down people's hearts is to make them feel miserable, and to squeeze all energy out of them. To pull up people's hearts is to make them greedy and ambitious, and thence prone to anger. When you are dealing with someone whose heart is hard, be gentle and sensitive; then gradually the heart will soften. When you are dealing with someone whose heart is soft, be firm and strong; then gradually the heart will harden. Thus every heart will find the right balance of softness and hardness.

* * *

There have been over the years many kings with many different ways of trying to exert control. Some have tried to manipulate people with cant about benevolence and righteousness. Some have tried to make people dependent on them by granting material gifts. Some have drawn up complex legal codes, threatening to punish those who did not adhere to them. Some have banished from their kingdom anyone who expressed dissent. Some have simply acted like robbers, imposing heavy taxes in order to accumulate wealth. All have failed. People have become discontented and angry, and so their kingdoms have been riven by conflict.

* * *

When yin and yang are out of balance, peace is overcome by fury; wisdom is overcome by folly; goodness is insulted by evil; sincerity is undermined by vanity; and the whole world degenerates. Nature and destiny break apart; people are so distracted that they ignore their own natures, and defy their own destinies. They thus become discontented. And to assuage their discontent they yearn for knowledge. Bad rulers rise up, forcing good rulers to hide in mountain caves. These bad rulers impose their authority with the saw and the axe, torturing and executing those who refuse to do their bidding.

* * *

A certain emperor ruled for nineteen years, and everyone obeyed his edicts. Then he went to see a wise man who lived at the top of a mountain. He said to the wise man: 'I have heard that you follow the perfect Way. I have come to ask you to teach me the perfect Way, so that I may bring blessings to all my subjects. I would like to learn how to balance yin and yang; and in this manner I shall enable my subjects to live in peace.'

The wise man replied: 'You think you are asking for harmony and peace. But in truth you are asking for even greater power over your people. This quest for power is upsetting nature, and ruining your people. The clouds rarely form, so rain rarely falls; the trees turn yellow before their fruit is ripe; and the sun and the moon grow ever weaker. Your heart has become numbed by the power you have wielded, and your body is becoming feeble. It would be a waste of effort to try and teach you the Way.

The emperor left the wise man, and gave up ruling his empire. He went to an isolated place, built a hut, and lived there for three months, without any human contact. Then he returned to the wise man. He approached the wise man on his knees, and repeated his request.

The wise man replied: 'I shall teach you the Way. The essence of the Way is hidden in darkness, lost in silence. Nothing can be seen; nothing can be heard.

64

Let your spirit be quiet and your body relaxed. Be still; be pure; do not struggle; do not disturb yourself. The eye does not see, the ear does not year, and the heart knows nothing. Yet your spirit guards your body, and your body will have a long life.'

The wise man paused, then continued: 'I will take you upwards to the sun, the source of light, the perfect yang. I will take you downwards to the place below the earth, the source of darkness, the perfect yin. Thus you will understand yin and yang. Hold them in balance, and everything else will take care of itself. You will have harmony within yourself, and harmony between yourself and all living creatures.'

The emperor bowed his head to the ground twice, and said: ' Master, you yourself are perfect yin and perfect yang; you are the Way.'

The wise man went on: 'People sometimes think they can see the Way, from its start to its finish; but no one can understand the Way in its entirety. Indeed the Way has no start and no finish. Those who truly follow the Way are kings and emperors. Those who see the Way, but do not follow it, are like the soil beneath our feet – the soil from which our bodies are made, and to which our bodies will return. Now you must go. And I shall continue my journey which has no end, towards the place where day and night are one.'

* * *

Actionless action is the only way of behaving which does not lead to disaster. On the contrary, if you practise actionless action, you will be transformed. Actionless action means disregarding the sensations of your body, ignoring what your ears hear and your eyes see, and forgetting that you are anyone. Then you will become one with the great void. Loosen the heart, and free the spirit; be calm, as if you had no capacity to be anxious. Be content with serene darkness; let the darkness surround you. Do not try to understand what I am saying, because this will cause you to reject it. Do not give my teaching a name, nor a shape.

11
AUTUMN FLOODS

———————◆———————

from *The Book of Chuang Tzu*, Chapter 17

The season of autumn came, when the skies opened. A hundred streams poured into the great river. The waters churned and swelled, breaking the banks. The low-lying land was covered, so the hills and mounts became islands. The livestock retreated to the islands for safety. Looking from one island to another, across the vast expanse, it was impossible to distinguish a horse from a cow.

The great river was very pleased with itself. In fact it was beside itself with joy. It was proud that it became the largest thing in the world, and now ruled most of the land.

Then the great river followed its own current eastwards. Eventually it reached an expanse of water far greater than itself, the great ocean. The river looked across the ocean, and could see no end to it.

The great river shook its head, sighed, and said: 'It is often said that people who have heard about the Way a hundred times, become proud. They think that, just because they know about the Way, they are following it – and hence are wise. I have been a victim of such pride. I have mocked the wisdom of those who are greater than me, and whose vision is wider. But now that I see the vast width of the ocean, I realise how foolish I have been. Indeed, if I had not come down to see the ocean, I would have been in great moral danger.'

Then the great ocean spoke: ' It is impossible to discuss my vastness with a frog in a well; his vision is limited by the space in which he lives. You cannot discuss ice with a summer insect; he only knows his own season. You cannot discuss the Way with a narrow-minded scholar; he is cramped by the knowledge that fills his mind. Some come out to the coast and see my vastness. Then they realise their own pettiness; and it becomes possible to discuss great principles with them.'

* * *

The great ocean continued its discourse: 'You cannot define the capacity of things; time never stops; there is nothing constant in human destiny; there are no fixed rules governing beginnings and ends. Thus great wisdom considers both that which is near, and that which is far off. It recognises that things which are small, are not always insignificant; and things which are large, are not necessarily more significant – because you cannot define the capacity of things. Great wisdom has a clear understanding of the past and present. It does not regard the past as remote from the present, nor does it strive to grasp the present – because time never stops. Great wisdom understands the nature of fullness and emptiness, and so is neither elated by success nor discouraged by failure – it knows there is nothing constant in human destiny. Great wisdom knows the straight and quiet road, so it does not rejoice in life nor regard death as a calamity – it recognises there are no fixed rules governing beginnings and ends.

* * *

'Calculate what a person knows; it is tiny compared with what that person does not know. Calculate how long a person is likely to live; it is tiny compared with the time before that person was born. Every aspect of our lives is tiny, yet often we regard things as tremendously important. This shows how muddled and confused we are. Look at it this way: how do we know that the tip of a human hair is the smallest thing possible?

Or how do we know that the universe can encompass the largest thing?'

* * *

'If a very small creature looks at a very large one, it cannot comprehend what it sees. Equally if a very large creature looks at a very small one, it can barely make it out. This suggests that, although it is convenient to distinguish between large and small creatures, their differences are merely a matter of circumstance. We may say the same about every distinction we make – such as coarseness and fineness. That which all things have in common, has no form, and hence no dimensions; thus it cannot be visualised, and cannot be described in words.'

* * *

Wise people do not set out to harm people, but equally make no display of benevolence or charity. They do not strive to make profits, nor do they consider servants and peasants as lowly. They do not haggle over the price of things, but happily abstain from what they cannot afford. They do not try to enlist the help of others in their work; nor do they make a show of their self-reliance. They are generous, but do not despise those who are greedy and mean. They are not influenced by fashion, but equally take no pride in being different from the crowd. They are self-effacing, but do not despise those who get ahead by flattery. They are not impressed by titles and worldly honours; but equally they feel no shame or disgrace when others treat them with contempt. They know that there is no fixed line between right and wrong, nor between great and small. They happily accept their destiny.

* * *

Following the Way brings neither fame nor wealth. Those who follow the Way lose all sense of self, so they have no interest in fame or wealth.

* * *

From the perspective of the Way, people are neither elevated nor lowly, noble nor mean. From their own perspective, people may make such judgements about themselves. But even common opinion says that individuals cannot be the judges of their own status.

Amongst different people, attitudes to status differ hugely. One person may ascribe high status to a particular quality or ability; but others will give equal status to ten thousand other qualities and abilities. Another person may treat a certain trait with contempt; but others will treat with equal contempt ten thousand other traits. We can grasp the confusion only if we regard a tiny grain and the tip of a hair as vast mountains.

* * *

A great wooden beam can be used to batter down a city wall, but would be no good for filling a small hole; this refers to two quite different functions. A thoroughbred horse may be able to gallop a thousand miles in a day, but as a rat-catcher it is no match for a cat or a weasel; that refers to two quite different skills. The horned owl can catch fleas at night and can spot the tip of a hair, but at dawn, no matter how wide it opens its eyes, it cannot see even a hill or a mountain; this refers to a difference of nature. So how can you say that you will always obey the rules of righteousness, and banish all that is wrong? How can you assert that good order will prevail, and disorder will be routed?

* * *

From the perspective of the Way, our notions of what is high and low, noble and mean, are subject to constant change. Do not cling to your ideas, because that is contrary to the Way. Concepts of status, and even concepts of quantity, are of very little use. Do not attempt to be a particular type of person, but be many types simultaneously. Be stern and strict, like a judge who favours no one. Be benign and gentle, never acting selfishly. Be as liberal and generous as the earth, not discriminating between people. Be kind and loving to every form of life. Regard all life as one.

* * *

The Way has neither start nor finish, neither beginning nor end. But all living creatures have a start and a finish: they are born, and they die. So you cannot put your trust in living creatures. One moment they are full of life, and the next moment they are empty. The years cannot be reversed, and the passage of time cannot be halted. Bodies grow and decay; they flourish and they wither. We may talk of eternal principles that underlie all life. But life itself is a headlong gallop, changing with every movement, and altering every minute. So what should you do and not do? You should go along with the process of change.

* * *

In order to understand the Way, people must understand its eternal principles. And those who understand these principles are able to handle every situation. They can ensure that they come to no harm. Those who truly follow the Way do not suffer through cold and heat; fire will not burn them, nor water drown them; birds and beasts cannot injure them. I do not say that they make light of these things. I mean that they are alert to safety and danger, fortune and misfortune; and so they are cautious in all they do.

* * *

The one-legged creature envies the millipede. The millipede envies the snake. And the snake envies the wind.

The one-legged creature said to the millipede: 'With only one leg, all I can do is hop. I make very slow progress. How on earth do you manage to co-ordinate the multitude of feet you possess? The millipede replied: 'You don't understand. I simply set the mechanism in motion. I do not know how it works.'

The millipede said to the snake: 'Although I have all these legs, I cannot keep up with you – who have no legs. How is that?'

The snake replied: 'I just move as I am supposed to move. I cannot alter the way I am. What would I do with legs if I possessed them?'

The snake said to the wind: 'Although I have no legs, I still have a body; and I must drag this body along the ground. But you can blow from the north, and disappear to the south, without any body. How is that?'

The wind replied: 'It is true that I move at great speed over great distances. But if you hold up a single finger against me, I must stop; and you can trample me under foot. Despite my weakness, I can uproot great trees, and blow down great homes; this is my most spectacular ability. Thus I turn all my little defects into a great victory.'

To turn defeats into victory, to turn weaknesses into strength – that is the mark of true wisdom.

* * *

For a long time I tried to avoid hardships and difficulties. I often failed; that is destiny. For a long time I tried to achieve success. I often failed; that is destiny. There may once have been a period when no one in the entire world suffered hardship or disappointment. But it was not this wisdom that protected them. There may once have been a period when no one enjoyed success. But it was not their lack of wisdom that thwarted them. Time and circumstance determine hardship and comfort, success and failure.

* * *

A wise man was walking with a friend along the bank of a river. The wise man exclaimed: 'Look at how the fish are darting hither and thither, going wherever they please. They are really enjoying themselves.'

The friend replied: 'You're not a fish. So you can't possibly know what a fish enjoys.'

The wise man said: 'You are not me. So you can't possibly know that I don't know what a fish enjoys.'

12

STRIVING FOR HAPPINESS

from *The Book of Chuang Tzu*, Chapter 18

Is it possible to enjoy perfect happiness in this world, or not? Is there some way of keeping yourself alive, or not? What can be done, and what is to be trusted? What should be avoided, and what should be welcomed? What should be pursued, and what should be abandoned? Where is goodness to be found, and where is evil?

* * *

People generally desire wealth, status, long life, and respect. They think happiness consists in luxury, fine food, beautiful clothes, delightful surroundings and sweet sounds. They despise poverty, ugliness, illness and disgrace. They dread a way of life in which the body has no rest, the mouth never tastes good food, the skin never feels soft clothes, the eye never feasts on bright colours and elegant forms, and the ear never enjoys sweet music. The fear of being reduced to such a way of life causes people much unhappiness.

How foolish! People who are rich wear themselves out accumulating riches; and they invariably acquire more than they need. People who are eminent spend their days and nights hatching plots, in order to enhance their power. So the rich and the eminent, far from attaining happiness, condemn themselves to lives of constant anxiety. Most die young; and those who survive into mature years, become confused and miserable. Only fools treat themselves in this fashion.

* * *

Most people make happiness their supreme goal. And they struggle hard to attain this goal; in fact, they never stop striving after happiness. Yet there is a paradox. Those who seek happiness do not find it. Those who make a distinction between happiness and unhappiness are never at peace – so they are never happy. As wise people have said: 'Perfect happiness is not happiness; perfect glory is not glory.'

The world is incapable of judging happiness and unhappiness. I regard actionless action as worthy of being called happiness. The world is incapable of judging right and wrong. Yet actionless action can determine right and wrong. Remaining alive is an essential condition for happiness; and actionless action is the best way to preserve life.

* * *

The wife of a wise man died. A friend came to offer his condolences. But he found the wise man sitting on the ground, beating a drum and singing. The friend exclaimed: 'You lived with her for many years, and she reared your children. The least you could do is to be on the verge of weeping. Yet here you are, beating a drum and singing. It's not right!'

The wise man replied: 'When she first died, I grieved as anyone else would. But then I thought back to her birth, and to the time before her birth – indeed, to the time before she was ever conceived, and before the breath of life entered her. From this state of nothingness, a wonderful and mysterious change occurred: she received a spirit. A further change occurred: she received a body. A further change occurred: she was born. Now another change has occurred: she has died. It is just like the progression of the four seasons, spring, summer, autumn and winter. She is now peacefully lying on her bed. If I were to sob and cry, it would show that I did not understand the ways of fate. That is why I am not sobbing and crying.' * * *

To live is to scrounge, taking what you can in order to survive. So, since living is scrounging, the result of our efforts is to amass a pile of rubbish.

* * *

A bird with beautiful feathers flew over a city, and came down to rest in someone's garden. The owner of the garden was so enchanted with its beauty, that he caught the bird in a net. He took it to the main temple, where it could hear sweet music being played. He fed it meat which had been used in sacrifices, and he offered it wine that had been used in rituals. But the bird looked anxious and forlorn. It refused to eat any meat or drink any wine. In three days it was dead.

This was the result of trying to care for a bird as if it were a human. Birds must be allowed to live like birds, roosting in the forests, playing amongst the branches, swooping down to eat works, and flying in great flocks.

* * *

Fish need to live in water. But if humans were to try and live in water, they would die. Different creatures have different needs, different likes and dislikes. Thus wise people never expect the same from all creatures, and never try to make them live in the same way. Our concepts of right and wrong should depend on what suits each particular creature.

* * *

A wise man was on a journey, and was sitting on the roadside to eat his meal. He saw a human skull nestling in the grass. He put his hand gently on it, and said: 'Only you and I know that you never died, nor were you ever born. Are you really unhappy? Am I really enjoying myself?'

13
MASTERING LIFE

━━━━━◆━━━━━

from *The Book of Chuang Tzu*, Chapter 19

If you have grasped the purpose of life, you will not try to make life into something it is not, and cannot be.

If you have understood the nature of destiny, you will not try to alter destiny by acquiring knowledge.

If you wish to care for your body, you must have concern for material things. Yet it is possible to have all the material things you could possibly want, while the body remains unhealthy.

Since you have received the gift of life, it is important that life does not leave your body. Yet it is possible for the body to remain alive, while life itself is not worth living.

Birth cannot be avoided, and death cannot be prevented. Many people believe that simply by caring for the body, life can be indefinitely preserved. How foolish! They should learn that merely caring for the body is not sufficient to sustain life. The body should not be neglected, but nor should it be over-valued.

The best way to care for the body is to abandon worldly entanglements. If you are not entangled in worldly affairs, you will be virtuous and peaceful. In fact, you will be born again into a new form of living; you will be following the Way.

You will sustain life by forgetting life – life as it is lived in the world. By forgetting life your inner vitality will be preserved and enhanced. You will be unified with all that exists.

* * *

A disciple said to a wise man: 'It is said that those who are truly wise can walk under water without drowning, walk on fire without burning, and can encounter any living creature without being frightened. How do they manage this?'

The wise man replied: 'They guard their original, pure breath. This has nothing to do with wisdom or skill, persistence or courage. Sit down, and I shall tell you all about it.

'Every creature has its own face, form, voice and colour; but these are the outward aspects. Yet in truth one creature and another creature are not so different as their differing aspects would suggest. Although a creature's outward aspects may be unique, that creature cannot possibly be the first of all creatures. Thus its outward uniqueness is insignificant. It follows that all creatures originate from that which has no face or form, no voice or colour; they must originate from that which is changeless.

If you can truly understand this, and if your life can be transformed by this understanding, then nothing can stand in your way. You can reside within boundaries that have no boundary; you can be secluded in a land that has no border; you can ramble across the territory where life both begins and ends. You can live in harmony with your own nature; you can nourish the original breath of life within you; and thence you can commune with the origin of all life. Your spirit will have no flow or fault; so nothing will be able to attack you, from outside or from within.'

* * *

When a drunk falls out of his carriage, even though the carriage may be moving fast, he will not be killed. He has bones and joints like any other man; but he is not injured as they would be, because his spirit is not present at the accident. He did not know that he was in the carriage, and he is not aware that he has fallen out. Life and death, alarm and terror, do not enter his breast. Thus when he hits the ground, he is perfectly relaxed, and so is unscathed. If a person can keep himself whole by means of wine, how much more effective will wisdom be!

* * *

A hunchback was juggling in the market-place.

Someone asked him how, despite his deformity, he had learnt to juggle so well.

The hunchback replied: 'For six months I juggled with only two balls. For a further six months I juggled with three balls. And I added an extra ball every six months until I reached the maximum of seven balls. I know that my body is no better than a twisted old tree; and my arms are like withered branches. But my mind gradually learnt to concentrate solely on the balls I juggle, to the exclusion of all else. So how could I fail?'

* * *

A man crossed a wide, fast-flowing river on a ferry. The ferryman handled the boat with superlative skill. The man asked how he acquired this skill. The ferryman replied: 'A good swimmer will get the knack of it in no time. Someone who can swim under water will know exactly how to handle a boat – even if he has never seen one before.'

The man was perplexed by this answer; and a few days later he asked another man, renowned for his wisdom, to explain it. The wise man replied: 'A good swimmer will not be afraid of the water. Someone who can swim under water will treat water like dry land; so the ability which everyone has to steer a cart will be applied to a boat. Lack of fear and natural ability are sufficient for any task.'

* * *

When you are shooting crows for fun, your aim is excellent. When you are competing in an archery contest, with a prize for the winner, you are nervous; so your aim is less good. And the larger the prize, the worse your aim becomes. Your skill is the same in all cases. But when other considerations enter your mind – namely, thoughts of a prize – you become clumsy.

* * *

When people are about to set off on a journey, and news comes that many people are being killed by robbers on their route, then all their relatives will urge them to be careful; and they will arrange for an armed escort. They are right to be worried. But people should worry far more about the things that enter their head when they are alone, especially when they are lying in bed at night. These anxious thoughts are warnings; and we ignore them at our peril.

* * *

A priest spoke to his pigs: 'Why should you object to dying? For three months I'm going to fatten you up. Then I shall pray for nine days, and fast for three days. Finally I shall take you into the temple, and slaughter you as a sacrifice. Surely you are happy with that.'

The priest paused, and began to think: 'If I were planning things from the point of view of a pig, it would be better to remain here in the pen, eating chaff and bran. So speaking for the pigs, I would flatly refuse my proposals. I wonder why I perceive things so differently from a pig?

* * *

A man went to visit a famous waterfall, where the water falls from such a height that no fish can swim in the river below. This man was amazed to see another man dive into the rough water underneath the waterfall, and swim about two hundred yards. The swimmer then came out of the water, and strolled along the bank, singing a song.

The first man ran up to the swimmer, and exclaimed: 'At first I thought you were a ghost, but now I see you're a man. May I ask, do you have some special way of staying afloat in that rough water?'

The swimmer replied: 'I have no special way. I started with what I knew; I matured according to my nature, and I let destiny do the rest. I go under with the swirls, and come up with the eddies, following the way the water goes. I never think about myself. That is how I stay afloat.'

* * *

A woodcarver made the most beautiful objects, so that everyone marvelled at his skill. One day someone asked him how he set about carving an object.

The woodcarver replied: 'When I am making a particular object – such as this bell-stand – I do not let it wear me out. I begin by fasting, in order to calm my mind. When I have fasted for three days, all thoughts of praise and reward have left my mind. When I have fasted for five days, all pride in my own skill has left my mind. When I have fasted for seven days, I am entirely unaware of my limbs and my body. Thus my mind is wholly concentrated on the task; all distractions have faded away. After that, I go into the forest to contemplate the trees. Eventually I find one whose form contains the form of the object I wish to carve. Only then do I start carving.'

* * *

You forget your feet when your shoes are comfortable. You forget your waist when your belt is comfortable. You forget about right and wrong when your mind is comfortable. You forget about knowledge when you are comfortably following the Way. Regardless of what changes occur outside, you remain contented within. And true contentment consists in forgetting what contentment is.

14
THE HUGE TREE

from *The Book of Chuang Tzu*, Chapter 20

One day a wise man, accompanied by a disciple, was walking through a forest. They came to the largest tree in the forest; nearby was a woodcutter. The wise man asked the woodcutter why this huge tree had not been cut down. The woodcutter replied: 'The wood is useless, so there would be no point in cutting it down. In fact, that is why is has been allowed to grow so large.'

That night the wise man and his disciple arrived at a friend's house. The friend was delighted to see the wise man; and in the wise man's honour he ordered his son to kill a goose and cook it. The son said: 'We have two geese, one that cackles and one that is silent. Which shall I kill?' The father replied: 'Kill the silent goose. It's useless in warning us when strangers approach.'

The following morning the disciple said to the wise man: 'In the forest the useless tree is spared, while useful trees are cut down. But in your friend's house the useless goose is killed, while the useful goose is spared.'

The wise man laughed, and replied: 'It might seem that a position between being useful and useless would be safest. But that is not right; troubles would pursue you. Instead you should transcend this distinction between usefulness and uselessness. That is what is meant by following the Way.'

* * *

Here is how to follow the Way. Never be certain of what is right; never allow yourself to be directed by those who claim to be certain. Never be fierce like a dragon; never be wily like a snake. Behave in whatever fashion is appropriate to the situation. Let harmony be your guide. Float with the flow of life; allow all things to be as they are. Yet do not let others manipulate you, forcing you to think and act against your own nature. If you follow the Way, you shall be free.

* * *

In our time human life has become too complex. There are too many laws and moral codes telling us how to think and act. These laws and codes appear to foster unity; yet in truth they create division. They appear to help human beings to fulfil themselves; yet in truth they thwart human progress. They appear to elevate virtue; yet in truth they oppress the human spirit. They appear to be based on wisdom but they merely deceive fools.

* * *

The elegant fox and the graceful leopard live in the forest; that is where they are content. They are cautious creatures; so during the day they stay near their lairs, for fear of being seen by hunters. But at night hunger and thirst force them to go out in search of food and water. They plan their journeys carefully. Nevertheless occasionally they fall into traps or are caught in nets. What is to blame for their misfortune? Their own beautiful fur.

* * *

Do not trust your physical beauty or your charming manners. You should cast them aside as worthless.

* * *

There is a place where the people are fools, by the standards of the world. They want little and are content to live very simply. They know how to grow food for themselves; but they do not try to preserve food in case of poor harvests. They give away what they possess to those in need, and expect nothing back. They are ignorant of morality, and know little about religion. They are uncouth, and they dress in rags. At birth they are happy, and at death they are happy. Go and look for those people, and learn from them.

* * *

If a man is crossing a river in a boat, and is hit by an

empty boat, he will not be angry. This is because there is no one to whom he can direct anger. But if he is hit by a boat with someone inside, he will shout at that person to get out of the way. If the person does nothing, he will shout a second and a third time, using obscene and blasphemous words. At first he was not angry; but soon he works himself up into a wild fury. This is because he has a target for his anger.

Thus you must either learn to control your anger, or else live in a place so remote that you will encounter no one.

* * *

A king wanted new bells for his palace. So his collector of taxes decided to make these bells. He built a scaffold outside the city; and on the scaffold he cast the new bells, taking three months.

Someone asked him how he was successful both at collecting taxes and at casting new bells. He replied: 'My heart and mind are directed towards unity. So I do not dare try anything new. Being slow in thought, I do not understand what I do. Being tranquil in my emotions, I have no ambitions. I do not try to penetrate mysteries, or become familiar with what is strange. I let go what goes, and I welcome what comes. I pay attention to what cannot be ignored; and I ignore what cannot be grasped. I make friends with thugs and louts; I look after the humble and meek. And I avoid all arguments.'

* * *

There was once a bird who was utterly helpless. It had no strength in its wings; so when it tried to fly, it just flipped and flopped. Other birds had to help it. Thus when the flock was flying from one place to another, the helpless bird was never in the front or the rear; it was always in the middle. As a result, whenever the flock was attacked, the helpless bird was safe.

* * *

People drink first from the well with the sweetest water. So the well with the sweetest water is the first to run dry.

* * *

Those who are boastful rarely achieve anything worthwhile. Those who do worthwhile things usually see their achievements fade.

* * *

Those who have once enjoyed fame and success find it hard to revert to being ordinary citizens again. So those who follow the Way do not seek fame or success. They prefer to be obscure, to wield no power, and to achieve no success. They do not criticise others, so others do not criticise them.

* * *

Those who follow the Way can live among animals, and the animals will not be frightened. They can live among birds, and the birds will not fly away. So if animals and birds are not afraid of the Way, why should humans be?

* * *

A wise man was travelling with his disciples from one country to another. They stopped for the night at an inn. The innkeeper had two concubines, one beautiful and the other ugly. The ugly one was treated with great respect, while the beautiful one was made to serve the guests. The wise man asked why this was. The innkeeper's young son explained: 'The beautiful one is aware of her beauty, so we do not think of her as beautiful. The ugly one realises her ugliness, and so we do not think of her as ugly.'

The wise man turned to his disciples and said: 'If you know your faults, but think nothing of your talents, everyone will love you.'

15
COPING WITH THE WORLD

from *The Book of Chuang Tzu*, Chapter 26

When wood runs against wood, sparks start to fly. When metal is put in fire, it melts and flows away. When the natural balance is disturbed, we hear the crash and roll of thunder, and we see lightning flash across the sky, burning up whatever it strikes.

Happiness and sorrow are traps; and most people are caught between the two, unable to escape. They are anxious and fearful. They cannot concentrate on any task, so they bring nothing to completion. Their hearts are strung out, as if suspended between earth and sky. They are bewildered and deluded. Profit and loss rub against each other, starting countless fires which burn up human spirits. The moon cannot quench those fires. All is destroyed.

★ ★ ★

A wise man spoke so enigmatically that his disciples became frustrated with him. One day a disciple blurted out: 'Your words are useless.'

The wise man replied: 'You have to understand what is useless, before you can grasp what is useful.

The earth is broad and vast. An individual only makes use of a tiny portion of it. But if you were to dig away all the rest of the earth, leaving only that tiny portion, would the individual still make use of it?'

'No,' the disciple replied: 'it would be useless.' The wise man concluded: 'It follows that useless things have their uses.'

* * *

If people have an urge to travel, what can stop them? If people do not wish to travel, what can compel them? The former desire novelty, while the latter prefer conformity. But neither novelty nor conformity are compatible with perfect wisdom.

* * *

One person is a ruler, and another person is his adviser. But this is merely a matter of the times. Those who hold various titles change with each generation; and those who hold higher offices are no better than those who hold lower offices.

* * *

Those who are perfect leave no trace of their actions.

* * *

Wise people are able to avoid taking sides. They can work for others, obeying orders, without losing themselves. They prefer to listen than to teach. They are free of prejudice. So they first try to understand what people are saying – and only then make a judgement.

* * *

The eye that is penetrating can see clearly. The ear that is acute can hear clearly. The nose that is sensitive can distinguish smells. The mouth with a keen palate can enjoy different flavours. The heart that feels deeply has wisdom. And wisdom that is profound engenders virtue.

* * *

The great forests surpass humanity in their spirit. This is because human beings can act in a manner that is untrue to their natures. But trees always act in accordance with their natures.

* * *

A fish trap is used to catch fish; but once the fish have been caught, the fish trap is forgotten. The rabbit snare is used to catch a rabbit; but once the rabbit has been caught, the snare is forgotten. Words are used to express concepts; but once the concepts are grasped, the words are forgotten. I would like to find someone who has forgotten words; and I shall debate with that person.

95

FURTHER READING

The original English translation of *The Book of Chuang Tzu* appeared in 1891, by the pioneering scholar James Legge; it has been re-published by Dover Publications of New York. In 1996 Penguin, under its Arkana imprint, published a new translation of the complete text by Martin Palmer. Columbia University Press, also in 1996, re-published the earlier translation by Burton Watson of the seven Inner Chapters, plus four other chapters.